Extreme Weather

ANN O. SQUIRE

Children's Press®
An Imprint of Scholastic Inc.
New York Toronto London Auckland Sydney
Mexico City New Delhi Hong Kong
Danbury, Connecticut

Content Editor
Robert Wolffe, EdD
Professor
Bradley University, Peoria, Illinois

Library of Congress Cataloging-in-Publication Data
Squire, Ann, author.
Extreme weather / by Ann O. Squire.
  pages cm. — (A true book)
Audience: 9–12.
Audience: Grade 4 to 6.
Includes bibliographical references and index.
ISBN 978-0-531-20743-7 (lib. bdg. : alk. paper) — ISBN 978-0-531-21554-8 (pbk. : alk. paper)
1. Climatic extremes—Juvenile literature. 2. Weather—Juvenile literature. I. Title.
QC981.8.C53S68 2015
551.55—dc23   2014005461

All rights reserved. Published in 2015 by Children's Press, an imprint of Scholastic Inc.
Printed in China 62
SCHOLASTIC, CHILDREN'S PRESS, A TRUE BOOK™, and associated logos are trademarks and/or registered trademarks of Scholastic Inc.

1 2 3 4 5 6 7 8 9 10 R 24 23 22 21 20 19 18 17 16 15

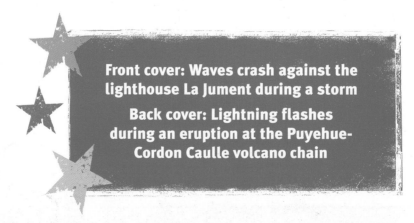

Front cover: Waves crash against the lighthouse La Jument during a storm
Back cover: Lightning flashes during an eruption at the Puyehue-Cordon Caulle volcano chain

Find the Truth!

Everything you are about to read is true *except* for one of the sentences on this page.

Which one is **TRUE**?

T or F Global warming causes more snow to fall during the winter.

T or F Hurricanes kill more Americans each year than any other type of extreme weather.

Find the answers in this book.

Contents

THE **BIG** TRUTH!

**Taking cover during
a hail storm**

Walking during a December 2012 blizzard

Tornadoes can destroy some buildings while leaving nearby buildings untouched.

5

About one percent of thunderstorms in the United States produce tornadoes.

CHAPTER 1

Out of a Thunderstorm

Have you ever been caught in a torrential downpour? Pulled the covers over your head during a thunderstorm? Woken up to find ice-covered trees and several feet of snow on the ground? If so, you know that weather can be unpredictable. It can also be violent and extreme. It can damage homes, buildings, and crops. Extreme weather is also responsible for many injuries and deaths every year.

Most tornadoes last a few minutes.
Extremely violent ones can last more
than an hour.

Tornado Watch

Extreme weather can take many forms. One of the
most dangerous weather formations is a tornado.
A tornado forms from a thundercloud. A spinning
funnel of wind reaches from the cloud down
to the ground. The funnel's whirling winds can
reach speeds of 300 miles (483 kilometers) per
hour. Because of their appearance, tornadoes are
sometimes called twisters.

Tornado Alley

Tornadoes can happen anywhere and at any time. However, some places get more than their share. One such place is the U.S. central plains, from South Dakota down to Texas. This region is nicknamed Tornado Alley. Tornadoes here occur most often in the springtime. The deadliest tornado in U.S. history struck here on March 18, 1925. It tore through Missouri, Illinois, and Indiana. Many towns were destroyed, and nearly 700 people were killed.

The March 1925 tornado left many buildings in ruins.

9

Why Are Tornadoes So Deadly?

Tornadoes are powerful storms. They can uproot trees, destroy buildings, and toss cars like toys. A tornado can be huge, with a path more than 1 mile (1.6 km) wide and 50 miles (80.5 km) long. Tornadoes develop very quickly and move unpredictably. This makes it hard to avoid a tornado, and people often do not have time to seek shelter. As a result, these storms kill many people every year.

Survivors in Joplin, Missouri, sort through debris left by a massive tornado that passed through the town in May 2011.

The more time a hailstone spends in a cloud, the larger it will grow.

Hailstones

Inside thunderclouds are strong drafts of warm air moving up and cold air moving down. A water droplet caught in an updraft is carried high in the clouds. There, it freezes into a tiny chunk of ice called a hailstone. A cold downdraft may push the hailstone lower, before an updraft carries it higher again. As the hailstone is tossed up and down inside the cloud, more layers of ice freeze onto it.

Hailstones can cause serious damage to cars and other objects.

Finally, the chunk of ice becomes so heavy that it falls to the earth. Most hailstones are only about 0.5 inches (1.3 centimeters) across or smaller. But strong, long-lasting thunderstorms are capable of creating large hailstones. These can be very dangerous and destructive. Imagine chunks of ice as big as baseballs hurtling out of the sky at more than 100 miles per hour (161 kph). You'll get an idea of just how damaging hail can be.

Deadly Hailstorms

Throughout history, hailstorms have been destructive. They are most dangerous in open areas, which offer little shelter. Hailstorms can also be deadly to animals and humans where homes and buildings are poorly constructed. In 1888, a strong hailstorm in northern India killed 246 people. Thousands of sheep, goats, and other farm animals also died. In 2001, a hailstorm hit St. Louis, Missouri. It caused nearly $2 billion worth of damage. This was the costliest hailstorm in U.S. history.

People in Melbourne, Australia, seek shelter from a severe hailstorm in March 2010.

Flash and Bang

Lightning strikes Earth an estimated 100 times each second. It occurs during thunderstorms, snowstorms, and dust storms. You might even see it flash in dust and gas erupting from a volcano. Lightning is extremely hot, sometimes reaching 50,000 degrees Fahrenheit (30,000 degrees Celsius). In October 2013, lightning in India killed more than 30 people in a single weekend. However, this was unusual. As common as lightning is, only one in about 10,000 people are struck by lightning in the United States in their lifetimes.

Lightning flashes in the cloud of ash erupting from Eyjafjallajökull Volcano in Iceland in 2010.

Anatomy of a Thunderstorm

A thunderstorm needs three things to form: warm, unstable air; moisture; and lift. Lift may be a mountain or wind. It pushes a mass of warm air high into the sky. As the air rises, it cools. Water vapor in it **condenses** to form a cloud.

As the thunderstorm grows, the air at the cloud top becomes positively charged. The air below carries a negative charge. The charge difference builds up. A giant spark of electricity jumps between clouds or to the ground to equalize the charge. This spark is lightning!

Men row down a street in Rui'an, China, that was flooded by rains brought by Typhoon Fitow in 2013.

CHAPTER 2

Windy and Wet

Whether you call it a typhoon, a cyclone, or a hurricane, you're talking about the same thing: a swirling tropical storm that forms over the ocean. When it makes **landfall**, a hurricane can wreak havoc. It carries high winds and heavy rain, and creates huge waves that cause coastal flooding. A hurricane is longer lasting and much larger than a tornado. After forming in the open ocean, most hurricanes become stronger as they move slowly toward land.

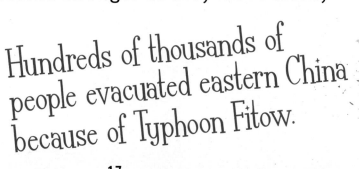
Hundreds of thousands of people evacuated eastern China because of Typhoon Fitow.

How Hurricanes Form

The recipe for a hurricane is simple: warm water, moist air, and wind. Hurricanes typically form near the **equator**, where the ocean water is warmest. The water heats the air above it. That air rises. Cooler air rushes in to replace it, then it warms and rises. Winds push the air around, and the storm grows. A hurricane is like an engine fueled by warm, moist air. It can grow as long as it is over warm water.

Hurricanes north of the equator spin counterclockwise. Those to the south spin clockwise.

Clouds spin around the eye of Hurricane Dean, which formed in the Atlantic Ocean in 2007.

A Giant Storm

At the hurricane's center is the **eye**. The air there is calm and clear. Outside the eye, wind speeds may reach more than 150 miles per hour (241 kph). Hurricanes can grow to be hundreds of miles across. In 1999, a giant hurricane named Floyd hit the eastern United States. Floyd's effects were felt from the Bahamas all the way to New England.

Hurricane Sandy caused a section of a boardwalk amusement park in Seaside Heights, New Jersey, to wash away.

Heavy Rain and Storm Surge

Hurricane clouds can dump many inches of rain in less than a day. What's more, the spiraling winds gather ocean water into a large mound at the center of the storm. This mound is called a storm surge. When the hurricane reaches land, the storm surge is pushed onto the coastline. A storm surge can flood low-lying coastal areas. In 2012, Hurricane Sandy brought a 32-foot (9.8-meter) storm surge that roared into New York Harbor.

Death of a Hurricane

When a hurricane reaches land, it's usually bad news for people living along the coastline. But it is also the beginning of the end of the storm. Hurricanes need a constant supply of warm, wet air to survive. When they reach land or colder ocean water, they stop growing. And when hurricane-force winds encounter land formations such as hills and mountains, they slow down. Soon, the hurricane dies out.

People experience high winds as Hurricane Sandy approaches the Massachusetts coast.

21

Hurricane Katrina

On August 23, 2005, a storm began to form near the islands of the Bahamas. As it moved northwest, the storm grew into a powerful hurricane that **meteorologists** named Katrina. The hurricane dumped many inches of rain in Florida before continuing into the Gulf of Mexico. Over warm ocean water again, the hurricane intensified. When it hit Louisiana, Katrina was 400 miles (644 km) across. Its winds moved up to 140 miles per hour (225 kph).

Hurricane Katrina did damage throughout the Southeast. New Orleans, Louisiana, was especially hard-hit. New Orleans is surrounded by water. Much of the land is below sea level. Engineers had built **levees** and seawalls to protect the city. But the rain and storm surge overwhelmed them. The storm surge reached 30 feet (9.1 m) high. Thousands of homes and buildings were destroyed. Nearly 2,000 people lost their lives.

People cool off in a fountain near the Eiffel Tower in Paris, France, during a heat wave.

CHAPTER 3

Heat Waves, Droughts, and Wildfires

Not all extreme weather involves rain. A heat wave consists of days or weeks of very high temperatures. High temperatures can cause faintness, nausea, confusion, and even unconsciousness. Organ damage or death may also occur. In the United States, heat results in more deaths on average than floods, lightning, tornadoes, hurricanes, or severe winter weather!

 Heat affects children and the elderly more severely than it does other people.

How Heat Waves Occur

A heat wave begins when warm air, called a high pressure system, gets stuck over an area of land. With no cool air coming in, temperatures rise. High pressure systems usually do not carry clouds. As a result, direct sunlight heats things up even more. Heat waves are usually more severe in cities. The concrete, asphalt, and metal in the streets and buildings hold the heat.

Parasols or umbrellas can offer shade from the heat of the sun during a heat wave.

Droughts in agricultural areas, such as portions of the U.S. Midwest, can damage crops.

Drought

People often complain when they wake up to a rainy day. But imagine having no rain for months or even years. The earth becomes dry and cracked, plants wither and die, and wildlife suffers without enough water to drink. Eventually, water levels in reservoirs and lakes decrease. Rivers and streams may dry up. This type of extreme weather is called a drought. Droughts and heat waves often go hand in hand.

By 1940, 2.5 million people had left their homes because of the dust storms.

The Dust Bowl

In a severe drought, the top layers of soil may dry up and turn to dust. Wind picks up the dust and creates blinding dust storms. This is what happened on the Great Plains in the 1930s, during a period called the Dust Bowl. Dust storms turned the sky black. In some areas, most of the soil was blown away. Farmers were forced to abandon their farms and look for work elsewhere.

Wildfires

Droughts and heat waves greatly increase the chance of wildfires. When there is no rain for a long period, soil, trees, and other vegetation dry up. Then it only takes a small spark to start a fire. Wind helps the fire spread. Before long, the wildfire is so large that it cannot be controlled. In many cases, not just forests, but also homes and buildings in the path of the fire are destroyed.

A large wildfire can produce its own wind as it builds.

A parent and child huddle together as they walk down the sidewalk through a blizzard.

Wild Wintry Weather

If you've built a snowman, sledded down a hill, and thrown snowballs with your friends, you know that winter weather can be fun and exciting. But cold weather can also be dangerous for your health. Heavy snow, strong winds, blizzard conditions, ice, and extremely cold temperatures are some of winter's dangers. This is especially true if you are not prepared for the weather.

Layers of warm clothing help protect a person from freezing weather.

 The 1888 storm is partly responsible for New York City's decision to build an underground subway system.

The Great White Hurricane

In March 1888, a surprise storm blanketed the northeastern coast of the United States with snow. It blocked roads and train services and shut down telephone and telegraph lines. High winds pushed the snow into drifts as high as 50 feet (15 m). In these days before accurate weather forecasting, people were unprepared for the storm's severity. More than 400 people died, 200 of them in New York City.

The Storm of the Century

More than 100 years later, in March 1993, another gigantic winter storm slammed into the East Coast. It dumped snow on a larger area than any other storm in recorded history. Nearly half of the U.S. population was affected. Snow fell from Canada down to Florida. The storm resulted in 310 deaths and between $6 billion and $10 billion in damage. Unlike many winter storms, this one had winds as strong as a hurricane's.

A New York City resident digs her car out of the snow during the winter of 1993.

Polar Vortex

Poised above each of Earth's poles is a polar vortex. These cyclones high in the atmosphere contain very cold air. Air currents crossing North America and Eurasia sometimes break up the North Pole vortex. This can push brutally cold air south. When this happened in March 2013, temperatures in parts of Europe were more than 18°F (10°C) below average. The following January, a weakened polar vortex sent North American temperatures plummeting about 35°F (20°C) below average.

Icicles form along a Lake Michigan beach in Chicago, Illinois, during frigid temperatures related to the polar vortex in 2014.

Severe winds cause an average of 51 deaths each year in the United States.

Windchill

The **windchill factor** combines air temperature with wind speed to predict how cold it feels outside. As wind speed increases, it takes heat away from your body. This makes you feel colder. If the outside air temperature is 15°F (–9°C) and there is no wind, you will feel as though it is just that temperature. But if the wind picks up to 20 miles per hour (32 kph), it will feel like –2°F (–19°C)!

A winter storm makes travel difficult and dangerous for pedestrians and people in vehicles.

Winter Storm Dangers

Heavy snow and ice can cause trees to fall and buildings to collapse. If power lines come down, homes can be without heat or electricity for days. When people go outside during or after a winter storm without proper clothing, they risk **frostbite** or **hypothermia**. Icy streets can result in car accidents or injuries from falls. Even clearing snow away is dangerous. Many people die of heart attacks brought on by the hard work of shoveling snow.

Staying Safe

The best way to protect yourself during any extreme weather is to be prepared. Listen to weather forecasts. Have an emergency kit that includes flashlights, batteries, extra clothing, and any medicines that you or someone in your family need. Make a plan with your family about how to contact each other in case you are not together when the extreme weather hits. Do not travel or go outside unless local authorities ask you to **evacuate** your home. Above all, don't panic!

Climate change affects weather and ecosystems everywhere, from Australian rain forests to Alaskan mountain ranges.

Extreme Weather and Global Warming

Scientists have recently noticed more instances of extreme weather. They are predicting that, in years to come, weather will become even more extreme. The cause? Global warming, which is the gradual warming of our planet. Because of global warming, ocean temperatures have increased by more than 1°F (0.6°C) over the last century. So hurricanes—fueled by warm, moist ocean air— have become stronger and last longer.

Earth's average temperature rose 1.1°F (0.6°C) in the 20th century.

Rising sea levels put coastal areas at risk of being permanently under the ocean.

Rising Sea Levels

Another consequence of global warming is higher sea levels. When water heats up, it expands. This causes ocean levels to rise. Warmer air temperatures are also causing polar ice caps to melt, which makes sea levels rise even higher. This is especially bad news for people living in coastal areas. Higher sea levels make these low-lying areas more prone to flooding by a hurricane's intense rain and storm surges.

Thunderstorms and Tornadoes

As Earth's atmosphere becomes hotter, it becomes moister and more unstable. These are the perfect conditions for thunderstorms to develop. Scientists predict that the severity of thunderstorms over the eastern United States will increase dramatically by the end of the century. Although tornadoes and hail come from thunderstorms, no one knows whether increasing thunderstorm activity will mean more tornadoes and hail as well.

People struggle to cross a street flooded by a severe rainstorm.

41

Hotter and Colder

As our planet warms, the number of hot summer days increases. This means more heat waves, droughts, and wildfires. Global warming also means more rain and more snow in the winter. As the polar ice caps melt, there are larger areas of open ocean. When that ocean water evaporates into the atmosphere, it can eventually turn into rain or snow. Many meteorologists believe that is why recent winters have been snowier, despite Earth becoming warmer.

Timeline of Extreme Weather

1888

A hailstorm in India results in the deaths of 246 people.

MARCH 18, 1925

A massive tornado causes destruction in portions of Missouri, Illinois, and Indiana.

What Can We Do?

As Earth's weather becomes more extreme, it's important to know what weather to expect in your area and to prepare for it. It is also important to learn all you can about global warming and how it is changing our climate. Global warming is caused, at least in part, by human activities. If we change those activities and work together, we may be able to save our planet from even more extreme weather. ★

JANUARY 2014

Temperatures plummet in parts of the United States when the northern polar vortex breaks up.

AUGUST 2005

Hurricane Katrina becomes one of the deadliest hurricanes in U.S. history.

OCTOBER 2013

Lightning kills more than 30 people in India during a weekend of storms.

Size of a typical raindrop: 1/100 in. (0.0254 cm) to ¼ in. (0.635 cm) wide

Number of thunderstorms that occur at any given moment around the globe: 1,800

Average number of people killed by lightning in the United States each year: 53

Lowest winter temperature ever recorded in the United States: –79.8°F (–62.1°C) in northern Alaska on January 23, 1971

Most snow in a 24-hour period: 75.8 in. (1.9 m) in Silver Lake, Colorado, on April 14 and 15, 1921

Number of acres burned by wildfires in the United States in 2012: More than 9 million

Did you find the truth?

T Global warming causes more snow to fall during the winter.

F Hurricanes kill more Americans each year than any other type of extreme weather.

Resources

Books

Fradin, Judith Bloom, and Dennis Brindell Fradin. *Tornado! The Story behind These Twisting, Turning, Spinning, and Spiraling Storms*. Washington, DC: National Geographic Children's Books, 2011.

Kaye, Cathryn Berger. *A Kids' Guide to Climate Change & Global Warming: How to Take Action!* Minneapolis: Free Spirit Publishing, 2009.

Tarshis, Lauren, and Scott Dawson (illustrator). *I Survived Hurricane Katrina, 2005*. New York: Scholastic, 2011.

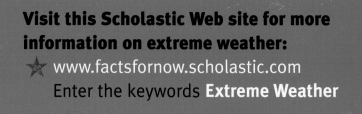

Visit this *Scholastic* Web site for more information on extreme weather:
★ www.factsfornow.scholastic.com
Enter the keywords **Extreme Weather**

Important Words

condenses (kuhn-DENS-iz) — turns from a gas into a liquid, usually as a result of cooling

equator (i-KWAY-tur) — an imaginary line around the middle of Earth that is an equal distance from the North and South Poles

evacuate (i-VAK-yoo-ate) — to move away from an area or building because it is dangerous there

eye (EYE) — the calm, clear area at the center of a hurricane

frostbite (FRAWST-bite) — a condition that occurs when extremely cold temperatures damage parts of a person's body

hypothermia (hye-poh-THUR-mee-uh) — reduction of the body temperature to an abnormally low level

landfall (LAND-fawl) — the time when a hurricane over the ocean hits land

levees (LEV-eez) — banks built up near a river to prevent flooding

meteorologists (mee-tee-uh-RAH-luh-jists) — experts in the study of Earth's atmosphere

windchill factor (WIND-chill FAK-tur) — a measurement given in degrees that reports the combined effect of low temperature and wind speed on the human body

Index

Page numbers in **bold** indicate illustrations

About the Author

Ann O. Squire is a psychologist and an animal behaviorist. Before becoming a writer, she studied the behavior of rats, tropical fish in the Caribbean, and electric fish from central Africa. Her favorite part of being a writer is the chance to learn as much as she can about all sorts of topics. In addition to the Extreme Science books, Dr. Squire has written about many different animals, from lemmings to leopards and cicadas to cheetahs. She lives in Long Island City, New York.